SLOANE'S

HANDY POCKET GUIDE TO

BICYCLE REPAIR

EUGENE A. SLOANE

A FIRESIDE BOOK
Published by Simon & Schuster Inc.
New York London Sydney Tokyo Toronto

A FIRESIDE BOOK
Published by Simon & Schuster Inc.
Simon & Schuster Building
Rockefeller Center
1230 Avenue of the Americas
New York, NY 10020
FIRESIDE and colophon are registered
trademarks of Simon & Schuster Inc.

Designed by Irving Perkins Associates, Inc.
Manufactured in the United States of America

1 2 3 4 5 6 7 8 9 10

Library of Congress Cataloging in
Publication Data
ISBN 0-671-66101-9

INTRODUCTION

NO MATTER how meticulously you've checked every bolt, nut, and bearing of your bicycle *before* a trip, you may still experience some kind of breakdown, since you simply can't anticipate when, where, and how a malfunction will occur. A breakdown that would be only a minor problem on home terrain could be a major disaster on a mountain trail, a remote country lane, or even a commute to work—unless you know how to solve the problem on the spot.

For example, a spoke may break miles from a bike shop. Brakes may fail at the most unexpected, white-knuckled moment. A derailleur may suddenly turn shiftless. Wheels once straight will become crooked and make accurate steering difficult. A chain might break so you can't pedal at all. Dirt may sneak into the free-wheel, causing movement in two directions so that the pedals move but the wheels don't.

This handy guide shows how to make emergency repairs on your bicycle when you're far from help, keeping repair time to a minimum and on-the-bike fun at a maximum. It is especially important to be able to cope with such problems when traveling in a foreign country where certain parts may not be available or where you can't communicate your particular needs to a non-English-speaking bike mechanic. Keep this troubleshooting book in your bike bag and you'll be able to consult it for expeditious repairs of flat tires and malfunctioning brakes, derailleurs, bearings, steering, transmission, and seating systems.

A WORD ABOUT TOOLS AND SPARE PARTS

I am going to assume that you *do not* have all the tools and spare parts I think you should take with you on an extended bike trip. Too many cyclists I have known have tried to make emergency repairs without the proper tools.

You will be able to deal with any mechanical quirk or failure much more quickly and with greater confidence if you do have the right tools and spare parts in your bike bag. Here are the tools and parts I recommend:

TOOLS

Tire lever
Brake third hand (for adjusting brake shoes and brake cable slack)

Small screwdriver

Chain breaker (for repairing, replacing, shortening, or lengthening a chain)

One set of thin cone wrenches to fit non-sealed wheel hubs (two 13–14mm or two 15–17mm wrenches; not needed for sealed-bearing hubs)

Spoke wrench

4 to 8mm Allen wrenches

4 to 15mm wrenches

Small adjustable Crescent wrench

Pair of pliers

SPARE PARTS

Four spokes to fit your wheels

Two extra long spokes to replace a rear wheel spoke on the freewheel side (see Problem 34)

Tire patches with patch cement and sandpaper

At least one extra tire tube

Small roll of duct tape to patch tube or tire slit

Tire pump

Small vial of 20 SAE oil

Pressure can of spray lube for the chain

Tube of bearing grease

One rear derailleur cable

One rear brake cable

Two brake shoes to fit your brakes

Six inches of chain links (identical to the chain on your bicycle)

A whole new chain for a long trip, such as one on a wilderness trail

BRAKE PROBLEMS

Let's start with brakes, because your welfare often depends on how well they work. Without brakes, your bike trip will come, so to speak, to an abrupt halt.

PROBLEM 1: Total brake failure. One or both brakes won't stop the bike at any speed, even when one or both brake levers come all the way to the handlebars or close to them.

Cause 1: The brake cable has slipped in the brake cable binder bolt. The cable is slack and will not actuate the brake shoes. (This problem is more common on all-terrain bicycles.)

Solution: Remove cable slack, tighten cable binder bolt, and readjust brake shoes, if necessary, as follows:

(a) Find the cable slack adjusters. They may be on the brake lever (Fig. 1), the brake arm (Fig. 2), the handlebar stem, the rear cable stop (Fig. 3), or on the front cable stop.

(b) Turn the adjuster barrel locknut ("L" in Fig. 1) counterclockwise as far as it will go, up to the adjuster barrel itself.

(c) Turn the adjuster barrel ("M" in

Fig. 1: This cable slack adjuster is located on the brake lever.

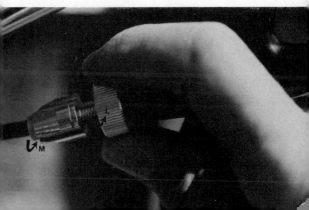

Fig. 2: This cable slack adjuster is located on the brake arm of a sidepull brake.

Fig. 3: A cable slack adjuster located on the rear cable stop of centerpull brakes. A similar adjuster is on the front cable stop of centerpull brakes.

Fig. 1) and the adjuster locknut clockwise as far as they will go.

(d) Hold, clamp, or tie the brake shoes tightly against the rim.

(e) Loosen the brake cable binder bolt located on the brake arm of sidepull brakes (Fig. 4) or on the cable carrier of other brakes (Fig. 5). Use one wrench to hold the bolt, another to loosen the binder bolt nut.

(f) Remove cable slack by pulling the cable tightly through the binder bolt.

Fig. 4: The brake cable is held in the brake cable binder bolt, here located on the arm of a sidepull brake. The lever on the right is a release that spreads brake arms apart so the wheel can be removed.

Fig. 5: The brake cable binder bolt on centerpull, canti-lever, cam, and U-brakes is located on the cable carrier.

(g) Tighten the cable binder bolt nut.

(h) Test binder bolt nut tightness by pulling on the brake lever(s) as hard as possible. If the cable slips in the binder bolt, repeat the previous steps.

(i) Make sure the brake shoe is about ⅛ inch from the rim flat (Fig. 6). If not, repeat steps (e) through (h) and add or remove slack as necessary. Use the adjuster barrel to fine-tune brake shoe-to-rim clearance.

(j) Make sure the brake shoe is about ⅟₃₂ inch below the top of the rim. If necessary, loosen the brake shoe binder bolt nut (Fig. 7) and set the shoe up or down as necessary, parallel to the rim.

Cause 2: Broken brake cable.

Solution 1: If you don't have a spare cable:

(a) If the front brake cable breaks, remove the rear brake cable and in-

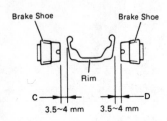

Fig. 6: Adjust brake shoes so they are ⅛ inch from the rim flats and about ⅟₃₂ inch below the top of the rim.

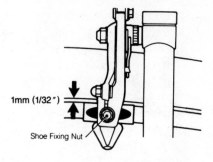

1mm (1/32″)

Shoe Fixing Nut

Fig. 7: The brake shoe binder bolt holds the brake shoe on the brake arm.

stall it on the front brake (80 percent of total braking power is from the front brake). See Solution 2 for cable installation instructions.

(b) Ride slowly, keep speed well under control downhill, buy a new cable, and replace the rear one as soon as possible.

(c) If the rear cable breaks, remove it and ride slowly until you can replace it with a new cable.

Solution 2: If you have a spare cable:

(a) Loosen the brake cable binder bolt (Fig. 4 or 5) and pull the cable from it.

(b) Pull the leaded bell end of the cable out of the brake lever on road bikes, as shown in Fig. 8, or out of the brake lever on an all-terrain bicycle, as shown in Fig. 9.

(c) Install a new cable and readjust the brake shoes as previously described.

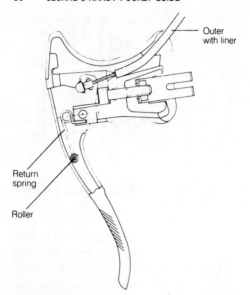

Fig. 8: Put the bell end through the slot in the brake lever, then push the rest of the cable through the lever into the spaghetti tubing.

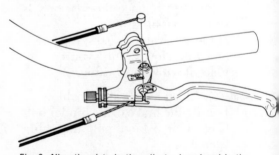

Fig. 9: Align the slots in the adjuster barrel and in the brake lever, then insert the leaded end of the cable in the brake lever and the cable into the spaghetti tubing.

Caution: Extension levers (Fig. 10) are designed for mild braking only. If you use them in an emergency they will not stop you in time to avoid an accident.

Cause 3: A brake pad popped out of the open end of a brake shoe (Fig. 11).

Solution: Find and replace the brake pad, or install a new one.
(a) Loosen the brake shoe binder nut.
(b) Rotate the brake shoe so the open end faces toward the rear of the bicycle.

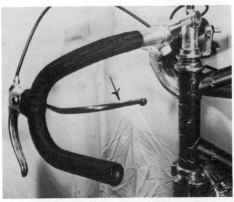

Fig. 10: Do not depend on extension levers to stop in an emergency. Use them only for routine braking.

Fig. 11: The open end of this type of brake shoe *must* face the rear of the bicycle.

(c) Tighten the brake shoe binder nut. *Note:* Mavic shoes have one end open. Other brake shoes have both ends closed.

Cause 4: Loose brake shoe binder bolt.

Solution: Tighten the brake shoe binder bolt as noted above.

> Caution: If the brake shoe rubs on the tire, the brake could lock and cause an accident. If a cantilever brake shoe binder bolt is loose, the brake shoe could dive under the rim and cause loss of braking power from that brake.

PROBLEM 2: Poor braking.

Cause 1: The brake cable has stretched so that the brake shoes are too far from the rim. This problem is most likely to occur on a new bicycle.

Solution: Remove cable stretch and readjust brake shoes as shown in instructions for Problem 1.

Cause 2: Brake shoes are worn down or have become age-hardened and have lost their friction grip.

Solution 1: If you have spare brake shoes, install them as follows:
(a) Loosen the brake shoe binder bolt (Fig. 7).
(b) Install new brake shoes and adjust their clearance from the rim. See Problem 1, Fig. 6.

Solution 2: If you don't have spare brake shoes, ride slowly and carefully to the nearest bike shop for replacements and install as above.

Solution 3: Check the rear brake shoes to see if they are in better shape than the front ones. If so, switch them. Remember, the front brake provides 80 percent of your braking power. Again, brake with greater caution, anticipate braking needs sooner, and go downhill more slowly until you have installed fresh new brake shoes.

Cause 3: Brake shoes are farther from the rim because ATB handlebars were lowered.

Solution: Readjust brake shoe clearance as in instructions for Problem 1.

Cause 4: Directional brake shoes are installed backward.

Solution: Reverse the position of the brake shoes so that the directional arrow on the brake pad faces the front of the bike (Fig. 12).

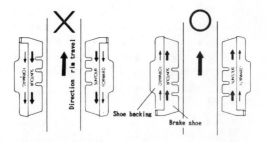

Fig. 12: The arrow on directional brake shoes must point toward the front of the bicycle.

(a) Loosen the brake shoe binder bolt.
(b) Rotate the brake so the directional arrow points toward the front of the bicycle.
(c) Check and if necessary readjust the brake shoe-to-rim clearances and alignment as in Problem 1, Fig. 6.

Cause 5: A brake shoe binder bolt has loosened and the brake shoe has moved out of position. If the brake shoe rubs on the tire instead of the rim, the wheel could lock when you brake. If a cantilever brake shoe gets under the rim, it could tangle in the spokes.

Solution: Tighten the brake shoe. If necessary, readjust the brake shoe-to-rim clearance as shown in solution to Problem 1.

Cause 6: Wheel is out of line, so both brake shoes do not contact the rim at the same time.

Solution: Check the wheel alignment. An out-of-line wheel will rub on one or both brake shoes. Lift the wheel off the ground, spin it and watch to see if the wheel rim moves closer to and then farther away from one or both brake shoes. If it does, realign the wheel as follows:

(a) Look at Fig. 13. Note that you can move the wheel rim to the left by tightening a left spoke nipple (counterclockwise) or by loosen-

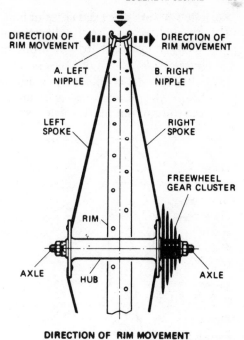

Fig. 13: An out-of-line wheel cuts braking power. Tighten a left spoke to pull the rim left and a right side spoke to pull it right, as shown here.

ing a right spoke nipple (clockwise). To move the wheel rim to the right, tighten a right spoke nipple or loosen a left one.

(b) Mark the rim where it's out of line and tighten the appropriate spoke nipple with a spoke wrench. If you can't tighten that nipple, loosen a nipple on the opposite side spoke. If you don't have a spoke wrench, use a small adjustable wrench or a pair of pliers.

PROBLEM 3: A brake shoe drags on the rim.

Cause: Brake arms are misaligned.

Solution: Loosen the brake binder bolt (Fig. 14) and move the brake so both shoes are the same distance from the rim. Re-tighten the binder bolt.

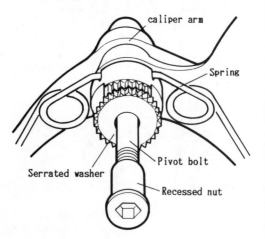

Fig. 14: The brake pivot bolt goes through the fork crown on a front brake and through the brake bridge on the rear brake.

PROBLEM 4: Both front brake shoes drag on the rim.

Cause: The brake shoes are too close to the rim because ATB handlebars were raised.

Solution: Loosen the brake cable binder bolt (Fig. 5) and let out enough cable so you can readjust the brake shoe-to-rim clearance as shown in solution to Problem 1.

PROBLEM 5: Brakes squeal.

Cause 1: Brake shoes are not toed-in.

Solution 1: Toe brake shoes in as follows:
(a) If your brakes have offset washers (Fig. 15), hold the binder bolt with an Allen wrench and loosen the binder nut with a wrench.
(b) Adjust the brake shoe toe-in so the rear of the brake shoe is farther from the rim (Fig. 15).
(c) Retighten the brake shoe binder bolt.

Solution 2: If your brakes do not look like the ones in Fig. 15, they do not have offset washers. Adjust toe-in by gently twisting the brake arm with a wrench.

Cause 2: A foreign substance is embedded in the brake shoe.

Solution: Remove the embedded particles or replace the brake shoe.

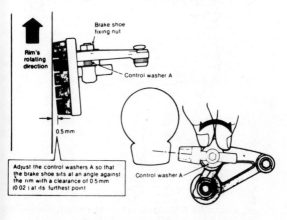

Rim's rotating direction

Brake shoe fixing nut

Control washer A

0.5 mm

Adjust the control washers A so that the brake shoe sits at an angle against the rim with a clearance of 0.5 mm (0.02˝) at its furthest point

Control washer A

Fig. 15: If a brake squeals, toe the front of the brake shoe in closer to the rim.

SHIFTING PROBLEMS

A recalcitrant derailleur is one of the more frustrating problems to beset a cyclist. In this section you will learn how to diagnose and then fix the most common gear-shifting malfunctions (even some uncommon ones) that could slow a trip to a crawl or bring it to a halt. Since a gear-shifting problem is easy to pinpoint as coming from either the rear or front derailleur, I have addressed the two possibilities separately. Let's start with the rear derailleur, source of most shifting troubles.

The Rear Derailleur

PROBLEM 6: The chain jams between the free-wheel and the rear wheel spokes.

Cause: Chain overshifts to the left.

Solution: Readjust the rear derailleur as follows:

(a) Lift the chain back onto the big freewheel cog (low gear). Use a screwdriver, camping knife, or similar tool to pry the chain loose if it's tightly wedged between the freewheel and the spokes.

(b) Move the rear derailleur shift lever slightly toward the smaller freewheel cogs (high-gear position).

(c) Turn the low-speed adjuster screw (Fig. 16) clockwise until the chain is aligned under the big freewheel cog (Fig. 17).

Fig. 16: The low-speed adjuster is closer to the freewheel than the high-speed adjuster, as shown here. Derailleur movement to the left is limited by the low-speed adjuster, and to the right by the high-speed adjuster.

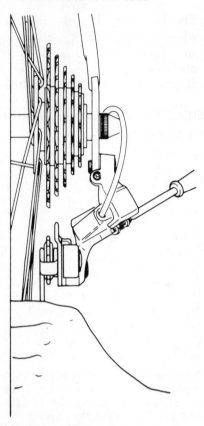

Fig. 17: Low-speed adjustment is correct when the chain is under the big freewheel cog.

(d) Lift the rear wheel off the ground, turn the cranks, shift the chain to the small rear cog, and then shift it rapidly back to the big cog. If the chain still overshifts to the left, repeat step **c** until the chain lands squarely on the big rear cog when you shift to low gear.

(e) Check the spokes on the free-wheel side for damage such as cuts and gouges from the chain. Replace damaged spokes as shown in directions for Problems 33 and 34.

PROBLEM 7: Chain won't shift to the biggest free-wheel cog (low gear).

Cause 1: The cable has stretched.

Solution: Remove cable slack and re-adjust the rear derailleur as follows:

(a) Shift the chain onto the smallest rear cog (high gear).

(b) Loosen the cable binder bolt, "2" in Fig. 18, at the rear derailleur.

(c) Pull the cable through the binder bolt and tighten that bolt.

(d) Hold the rear wheel off the ground, turn the cranks, and shift the chain to the big rear cog. Make minor adjustments with the low-gear adjuster, as in directions for

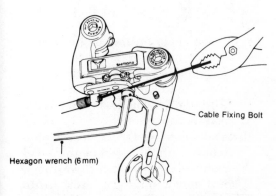

Cable Fixing Bolt

Hexagon wrench (6 mm)

Fig. 18: Loosen derailleur cable binder bolt, arrow, pull excess cable through binder bolt, tighten binder bolt.

Problem 6, so the chain lands squarely on the big cog when you shift to it.

Cause 2: The chain is on the big (high-gear) chainwheel, too short to fit on the biggest freewheel cog and the biggest chainwheel at the same time.

Solution: Shift the chain to a smaller chainwheel before shifting to a bigger freewheel cog. (*Note:* You may not be able to use the two biggest gears at the same time on some super-wide-ratio hill-climbing gears. That's because a chain long enough to be on the big rear and big front cogs at the same time would be too long and loose on other gear combinations.)

Cause 3: The chain is too short on close-ratio gears (13- to 24-teeth cogs on the freewheel, for example) or on moderate-ratio gears (14- to 32-teeth cogs on the freewheel).

Solution: Add one or two links to the chain.

(a) Use a chain breaker tool to install one or two more chain links. See Problem 48 for instructions on using the chain breaker tool. See (b) and (c) below to determine the correct chain length.

(b) The chain is the correct length when, with the chain on the small rear cog and the small chainwheel, the derailleur is perpendicular to the ground (Fig. 19).

(c) The chain is the correct length when, with the chain on the big

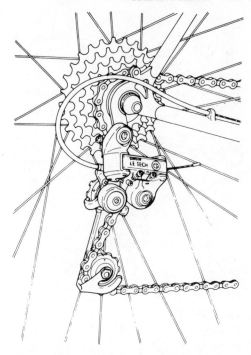

Fig. 19: The chain is the correct length when the derailleur is perpendicular to the ground and the chain is on the small rear and front cogs.

freewheel cog and the big chainwheel, the derailleur is parallel or nearly parallel to the ground (Fig. 20).

Cause 4: A broken derailleur cable.

Solution 1: Install a new cable.
(a) Move the rear derailleur shift lever to the high-gear position.
(b) Put the chain on the rear high gear (small cog), by hand if necessary.
(c) Turn the cable binder bolt (Fig. 18) counterclockwise and remove

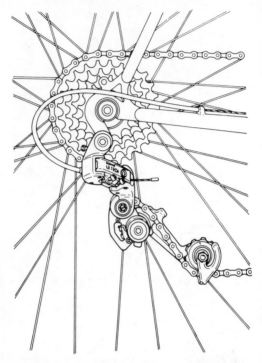

Fig. 20: The chain is also the correct length when the derailleur is horizontal and the chain is on the large rear and front cogs.

the broken cable from the derailleur. Remove the other section of the cable from the shift lever.

(d) Install a new cable through the shift lever and into the derailleur cable binder bolt.

(e) Pull the cable taut and tighten the cable binder bolt.

(f) Lift the rear wheel off the ground, turn the cranks, and shift to the low rear (big) cog.

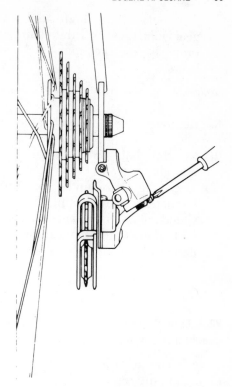

Fig. 21: High-speed adjustment is correct when the chain is centered under the small rear cog.

(g) Turn the low-gear adjuster (Fig. 16) until the chain is directly under the big freewheel cog (Fig. 17).

(h) Shift the chain to the high-gear (small) freewheel cog.

(i) Turn the high-speed adjuster (Fig. 16) until the chain is directly under the smallest freewheel cog (Fig. 21).

(j) Check shifting and make minor adjustments to the high- and low-gear adjusters until the chain sits properly on the high and low gears.

Solution 2: If you don't have a spare cable:

(a) Remove the broken cable as above.

(b) Put the chain on an intermediate rear gear.

(c) Align the chain under the intermediate gear by turning the high-speed adjuster. The chain will stay on that gear until you can install a new cable.

PROBLEM 8: The chain won't shift to the smallest freewheel cog (high gear).

Cause 1: The derailleur won't move far enough to the right.

Solution: Readjust the high-gear adjuster:

(a) Move the rear derailleur shift lever to the high-speed position.

(b) Put the chain on the small cog, by hand if necessary.

(c) Align the chain under the small cog (Fig. 21) by turning the high-speed adjuster (Fig. 16).

(d) Lift the rear wheel off the ground, turn the cranks, and shift the small cog up and then back. If the chain still won't go to the small cog, see the solution for Cause 2.

Cause 2: The cable is too short.

Solution: Lengthen the cable:
(a) Move the shift lever to the high-speed position.
(b) Put the chain on the small cog.
(c) Loosen the cable binder bolt and push about ⅛ inch of the cable up through the binder bolt. The cable in effect will be ⅛ inch longer between the binder bolt and the shift lever than it was before.
(d) Turn the high-speed adjuster as necessary until the chain is under the small cog (Fig. 21).
(e) Lift the rear wheel off the ground, turn the cranks, and shift the chain to the big (low-gear) cog and back down to the small cog. If the chain still does not go all the way to the small cog, repeat the adjustments in (c) and (d).

PROBLEM 9: The chain jams between the small freewheel cog and the chainstay.

Cause: The chain overshifts to the right.

Solution:
(a) Move the shift lever to the high-speed position.
(b) Put the chain back on the small cog. Pry the chain free if it has become jammed between the small cog and the chainstay. Use a screwdriver if necessary.

(c) Turn the high-speed adjuster (Fig. 16) clockwise until the chain is aligned with the small cog (Fig. 21). Check shifting as in Problem 8. Readjust the high-gear adjuster as necessary until the chain will move accurately to the small cog without overshifting off that cog and jamming between the cog and chainstay.

PROBLEM 10: The chain shifts by itself.

Cause: The shift lever is loose.

Solution: Turn the shift lever nut (Fig. 22) clockwise until it's tight. Make this adjustment on *both* shift levers. Avoid unwanted gear shifts that could cause loss of control and accidents by checking their tightness every few days when you're on a long trip.

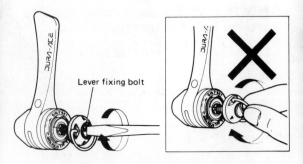

Lever fixing bolt

Fig. 22: Tighten the shift lever nut to prevent unwanted and unexpected gear shifts.

PROBLEM 11: The chain skips on freewheel gears.

Cause 1: There's not enough chain wraparound.

Solution 1: Adjust the rear derailleur chain tension screw.

(a) The chain should be on about half the teeth of any rear cog, "1" in Fig. 23. If the chain is on fewer teeth, "2" in Fig. 23, it can skip, cause loss of control and an accident.

(b) Shift the chain to the big (low-gear) rear cog.

(c) Increase chain tension by turning the rear derailleur chain tension screw (Fig. 24) counterclockwise until the chain is about ⅛ inch from the gear. *Note:* Some derailleurs do not have a tension adjuster.

Fig. 23: Correct chain wrap-around prevents chain skip and erratic shifting.

Fig. 24: Adjust the chain tension screw to move the chain closer to the gear for greater chain wrap-around.

Solution 2: Remove one or two chain links.
(a) See Problem 48 for using the chain breaker tool.
(b) See Cause 3 in Problem 7 for determining the correct chain length.

Solution 3: Move the rear wheel back farther in the dropouts.
(a) Turn the quick-release lever to the open position or loosen the axle nuts.
(b) Pull the wheel back as far as possible in the dropouts.
(c) Center the wheel between the chainstays and the seat stays.
(d) Turn the quick-release lever to the closed position or tighten the axle nuts.

Caution: Please read Problem 29, Cause 5 on the correct, safe use of the quick-release mechanism!

Cause 2: Worn freewheel cog teeth.

Solution: You probably won't be able to replace a worn cog (Fig. 25) on the road. Use the other four or five freewheel cogs and avoid using the worn one. Remember, chain skip can cause loss of control and an accident.

Cause 3: Worn, stretched chain.

Solution: Check the chain for wear.

(a) Replace the chain if it looks like the bottom one in Fig. 26. See Problem 7, Solution 2 for correct chain length and Problem 48 for use of the chain tool.

Fig. 25: Worn freewheel cogs, such as shown here, cause chain skip that can lead to loss of control and accidents.

Fig. 26: A worn chain also causes chain skip. Here the chain with the greater bend is the most worn and should be replaced.

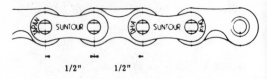

Fig. 27: Another way to measure chain wear is to count off 24 links. If the distance between the first and the 24th link is 12¹⁄₁₆ inch or greater, the chain should be replaced.

(b) Replace the chain if the distance between 24 links is greater than 12¹⁄₁₆ inches (Fig. 27).

(c) If chain skip is bad and you don't have a spare chain, use less pedal pressure (go slower) until you can install a new chain.

PROBLEM 12: You can't shift the rear derailleur.

Cause 1: The rear derailleur has been damaged.

Solution 1: Straighten a bent rear derailleur cage (Fig. 28) with a small adjustable wrench or twist it with a screwdriver until it's straight enough to let you shift.

Solution 2: If you can't repair the derailleur:

(a) Remove the chain. See instructions for Problems 9 and 48.

(b) Remove the derailleur with a 5 or 6mm Allen wrench (Fig. 29).

(c) Put the chain on an intermediate rear gear.

Fig. 28: A derailleur cage can be bent by hitting a curb or dropping the bike on its side. Straighten the cage, arrow, with an adjustable wrench.

(d) Shorten the chain. Remove enough links so it will stay on the intermediate gear. The chain should have about ¼ inch of up or down play.

(e) You still have two speeds if you have a dual chainwheel, or three speeds if you have a triple chainwheel set. You may have to strain

Fig. 29: Use a 6mm Allen wrench to remove the derailleur from the dropout.

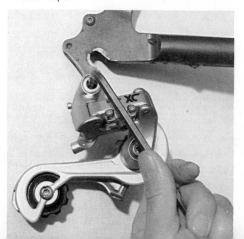

and huff and puff some—or walk up steep hills—but you'll get home or to a bike shop.

Cause 2: The rear derailleur cable is broken.

Solution: Replace the cable:
(a) Loosen the cable binder bolt (Fig. 18) and remove the cable. Remove the cable from the shift lever.
(b) Install a new cable. Pull it tight to remove cable slack and tighten the cable binder bolt on the derailleur. Readjust derailleur travel if necessary. See Problem 2.

If you don't have a spare cable:
(a) Remove the broken cable as above.
(b) Put the chain on an intermediate rear gear.
(c) Lock the derailleur in position by tightening both high and low adjusters (Fig. 16) as far as possible.

PROBLEM 13: The chain is noisy.

Cause: Inaccurate chain shift to a freewheel cog.

Solution: Move the rear shift lever slightly one way or the other until the noise disappears (i.e., until the chain is seated accurately on the freewheel cog of your choice).

PROBLEM 14: Inaccurate, noisy shifting on an index shift system.

Cause: The rear derailleur cable has stretched.

Solution 1: Turn the shift lever from the index to the friction mode (Fig. 30) and shift manually until you have time to work on the system.

Solution 2:
(a) Remove cable slack as shown in instructions for Problem 7.
(b) Make touch-up adjustments with the cable tensioner (Fig. 31).
(c) Adjust rear derailleur travel as shown in solution to Problems 7 and 8, if necessary.

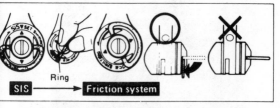

Fig. 30: Turn the index derailleur shift lever to the manual mode if the index mode malfunctions.

Fig. 31: Make fine-tune adjustments of cable stretch with the index system cable tensioner, shown here.

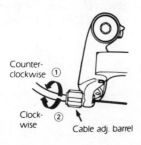

PROBLEM 15: The chain binds in the bottom (idler) rear derailleur pulley.

Cause: An open cage on the derailleur idler wheel lets the chain slip off that wheel.

Solution:

(a) Some derailleurs have an openable cage on the idler wheel (Fig. 32) so the chain can be removed from the derailleur without taking the chain apart.

(b) Close the cage.

(c) Tighten the pulley axle bolt.

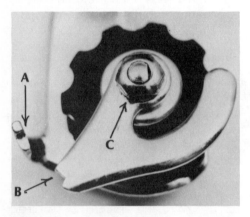

Fig. 32: Some rear derailleurs have an openable cage, shown here, to ease chain removal. Keep this cage closed and the cage binder bolt tight when pedaling.

The Front Derailleur

PROBLEM 16: Chain noise or rattle in the front derailleur.

Cause: The chain rubs on a front derailleur cage plate.

Solution:
(a) The chain angle inside the front derailleur cage (Fig. 33) changes when you shift the chain to a freewheel cog. If this angle change is acute, the chain can rub on the front derailleur cage.
(b) Keep the chain centered in the front derailleur cage by moving the front shift lever slightly one way or the other when you shift to another freewheel cog.

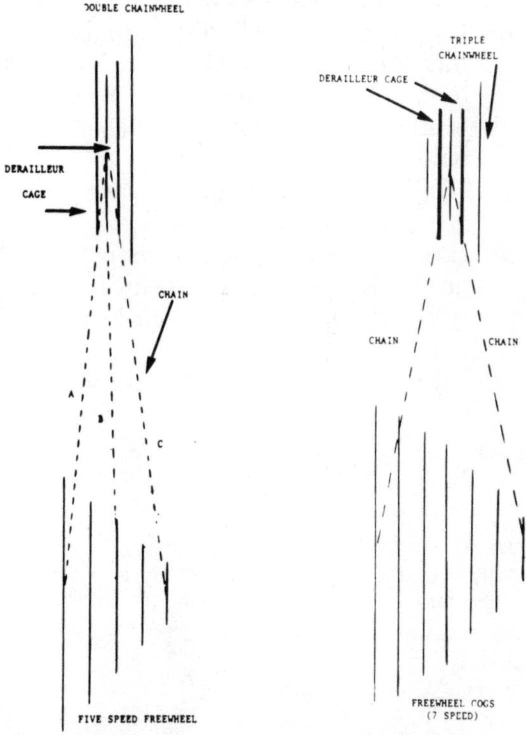

Fig. 33: Move the front derailleur shift lever slightly as you shift rear gears so the chain won't hit the inside of the derailleur cage. Otherwise, as you shift, the chain angle increases and the chain can hit the cage.

PROBLEM 17: The chain falls off the small chainwheel onto the bottom bracket shell.

Cause: The front derailleur low-gear adjuster lets the derailleur move too far to the left.

Solution: Readjust the derailleur travel to the left.

(a) Shift or put the chain back on the small chainwheel.

(b) Center the chain in the derailleur cage by turning the low-gear adjuster (Fig. 34) clockwise.

(c) Lift the rear wheel off the ground, turn the cranks, and shift the chain to the big chainwheel.

(d) Shift the chain to the small chainwheel. If the chain still falls off the small chainwheel, turn the low-gear adjuster one turn clockwise.

(e) If the chain still won't sit properly on the chainwheel, turn the low-gear adjuster counterclockwise one turn.

(f) Lift the rear wheel off the ground, turn the cranks, and check shifting.

(g) Readjust the low-gear adjuster as necessary.

Fig. 34: Use the high- and low-gear adjusters, shown here, to prevent the chain from overshifting off either chainwheel.

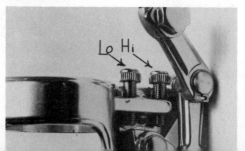

PROBLEM 18: The chain won't shift to the small chainwheel.

Cause 1: The derailleur won't move far enough to the left.

Solution: Readjust the low-gear adjuster (Fig. 34), as in solution to Problem 17.

Cause 2: The cable is too short, which prevents the derailleur from moving far enough to the left to shift the chain onto the small chainwheel.

Solution: Let more cable through the cable binder bolt:
(a) Loosen the front derailleur cable binder bolt (Fig. 35).
(b) Add about ⅛ inch of cable slack through the binder bolt.
(c) Tighten the binder bolt.
(d) Readjust the low-gear adjuster as in directions for Problem 17.

Fig. 35: Adjust front derailleur cable slack by loosening the cable binder bolt.

PROBLEM 19: Chain falls off the big chainwheel to the right, onto the crank.

Cause: The high-gear adjuster permits overshift.

Solution: Readjust the derailleur travel to the right:

(a) Turn the shift lever to the high-speed position.

(b) Shift or put the chain back on the big chainwheel.

(c) Center the chain in the derailleur cage by turning the high-speed adjuster (Fig. 34).

(d) Lift the rear wheel off the ground, spin the cranks, and shift the chain to the small chainwheel. Shift the chain back to the big chainwheel.

(e) Turn the high-speed adjuster one way or the other until the chain lands squarely on the large chainwheel without overshifting to the right.

PROBLEM 20: The chain won't shift to the big chainwheel.

Cause 1: The front derailleur cable has stretched.

Solution: Remove cable stretch.
(a) Move the front derailleur shift lever to the high-speed position.
(b) Loosen the front derailleur cable binder bolt (Fig. 35).
(c) Remove cable slack by pulling the cable through the binder bolt.
(d) Hold the cable taut and tighten the binder bolt.
(e) Check the high-speed adjuster as in directions for Problem 19.

Cause 2: Attempt to shift to big chainwheel while chain is on biggest rear freewheel cog.

Solution: See Problem 7, Cause 2. Before shifting to the big chainwheel, make sure the chain is not on the big freewheel cog.

PROBLEM 21: Erratic chain shift on both chainwheels. The chain does not always move to the selected gear.

Cause: Improper derailleur alignment.

Solution: Align the derailleur vertically and horizontally:
(a) Loosen the front derailleur clamp bolt (Fig. 36).
(b) Position the front derailleur so the outer (right) cage plate is about ⅛ inch above the big chainwheel and parallel to it (Figs. 36 and 37).

Fig. 36: The front derailleur cage should be about ⅛ inch above and parallel to the big chainwheel.

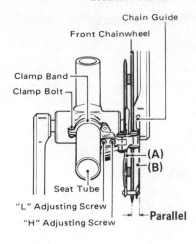

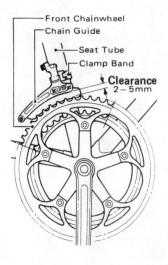

Fig. 37: Loosen the front derailleur clamp bolt, shown here, and move the derailleur as necessary for correct clearance and parallel adjustments as shown in Fig. 36.

PROBLEM 22: Chain skips on chainwheels.

Cause 1: Worn chainwheel teeth.

Solution: Use another chainwheel (of your double or triple chainwheel set) with teeth less worn until you can replace the original chainwheel. Chainwheel teeth should look like those shown in Fig. 38.

Cause 2: Worn chain.

Solution: See Problem 7, Cause 3.

Cause 3: Derailleur high- and low-speed adjuster settings.

Fig. 38: Teeth on a new chainwheel. If teeth are more worn than shown here, the chain can skip or jump off the freewheel.

Solution: See Problems 17, 18, 19, and 20.

Cause 4: Bent chainwheel.

Solution:
(a) Spin the cranks and mark where the chainwheel is bent.
(b) Carefully straighten the crank with an adjustable Crescent wrench (Fig. 39).

Cause 5: Derailleur horizontal and vertical alignment.

Solution: See Problem 21.

Fig. 39: Gently straighten a bent chainwheel with a wrench.

PROBLEM 23: Chain jams between chainwheels.

Cause: Loose chainwheel binder bolts that permit chainwheels to spread apart.

Solution: Tighten chainwheel binder bolts (Fig. 40). Hold the inner bolt with a chainwheel binder bolt wrench or a screwdriver. Tighten the outer nut with a 5mm Allen wrench. Tighten *all* the chainwheel binder bolts. (*Note:* Chainwheels are more likely to work loose on an all-terrain bicycle.)

Fig. 40: Use a screwdriver or special "L" wrench and an Allen wrench to tighten chainwheel binder bolts.

PROBLEM 24: Front derailleur shifts by itself.

Cause: Loose shift lever.

Solution: Tighten the shift lever nut (Fig. 22).

PROBLEM 25: The chain falls off the chainwheel on downhill runs. (It's most likely to occur on an all-terrain bicycle.)

Cause: Insufficient chain tension because the chain is on a small freewheel cog and a small chainwheel.

Solution 1:
(a) Increase chain tension by shifting the chain to a bigger freewheel cog *before* starting downhill. Or
(b) Leave the chain in the hill-climbing gear and shift to a higher gear after reaching the flats.

Solution 2: Increase the chain tension by turning the rear derailleur chain tension screw (Fig. 24) clockwise (if your rear derailleur has one).

TIRES

Potholes that punch a hole in the tire, sharp objects that puncture the tube, high-speed braking that heats the tube till it blows out, and low tire pressure that causes blowouts are just a few of the reasons a bike tire will go flat. Let's face it: you will, inevitably, get a flat tire. When a tire bottoms out you need to know how to repair it with a minimum of hassle and frustration. Fast tire repair may not be important on a long trip, but if you're commuting to work on your bike, time is essential.

Here's how to breathe air into your tube and keep it there.

PROBLEM 26: Flat front tire.

Cause: Punctured tube.

Solution: Repair the puncture, taking the steps below, depending on which type of brake is on your bicycle—cantilever, cam action, sidepull, or centerpull.

(a) Spread *cantilever* brake arms apart by squeezing the brake arms together and pulling the leaded end of the cross-over cable out of the brake arm (Fig. 41) so the flat tire can fit through the brakes.

(b) Spread *cam action brake* arms apart by squeezing the brake arms and pulling the cam out from between them (Fig. 42) so the flat tire can be removed.

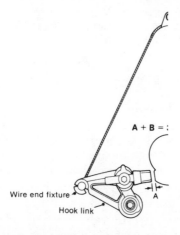

Fig. 41: Spread cantilever brakes so you can remove a wheel by removing the crossover wire from the brake arm, as shown here.

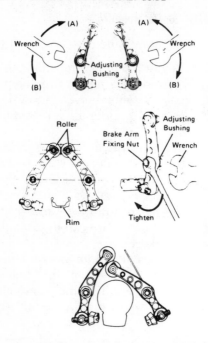

Fig. 42: Spread cam lever brakes apart so you can remove a tire by squeezing brake shoes and freeing the cam from between the brake arms.

(c) If you have *sidepull* or *centerpull* brakes, open the brake release (if you have one) so the tire will fit through the brakes. The brake release lever can be on the cable guide (Fig. 43), brake lever (Fig. 44), or the brake arm (Fig. 45).

(d) If your bicycle has a quick release unit on the hubs, turn its lever to the open position (Fig. 46).

Fig. 43: The brake release on sidepull or centerpull brakes can be on the cable guide.

Fig. 44: The brake release can also be on the brake lever.

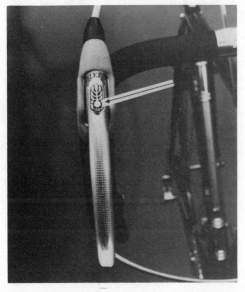

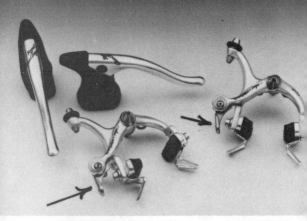

Fig. 45: Brake release on the brake arm of a sidepull brake.

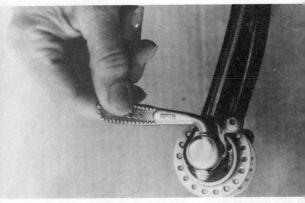

Fig. 46: Quick-release lever is in the open position.

(e) If the hubs are bolted on (Fig. 47), turn the axle bolts counter-clockwise until the axle is loose in the dropouts. Leave the axle nuts on the axle.

(f) Release any air remaining in the tube by removing the valve cap on a Schraeder valve (Fig. 48)

Fig. 47: A bolted-on axle hub.

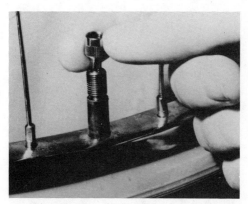

Fig. 48: This tube has a Schraeder (U.S.) valve.

and holding down the valve core,
or removing the valve cap of a
Presta valve (Fig. 49), turning the
valve core counterclockwise, and
holding it down.

(g) Remove the wheel from the fork
dropouts.

(h) Insert a tire lever between the

Fig. 49: A Presta
(European) valve tube.

tire bead and the rim (Fig. 50). If
you don't have a tire lever, use a
screwdriver or a quick release
lever. Be careful not to punch another hole in the tube as you use
these tools.

(i) Remove the tube from the tire.

(j) Pump up the tube. Find and
mark location of the puncture(s)
by dunking the tube in water
(Fig. 51), listening for the hiss of
escaping air (Fig. 52) or feeling
for escaping air (Fig. 53).

Fig. 50: Insert a tire lever between the tire and the rim
to remove a tire.

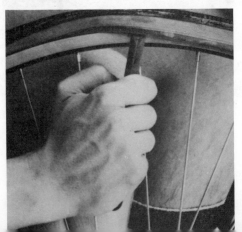

Fig. 51: Find leaks by inserting the tube in water and watching for bubbles.

Fig. 52: Check for leaks by listening for the hiss of escaping air.

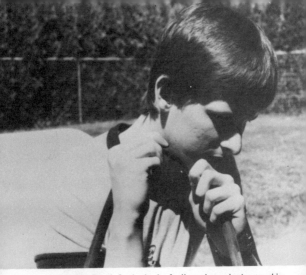

Fig. 53: Check for leaks by feeling air against your skin.

(k) Abrade the area around the puncture(s) with sandpaper (Fig. 54).

(l) Apply a few drops of patch glue on the abraded area (Fig. 55). Let it get tacky.

(m) Peel the protective wrap from a tube patch. Press the patch down over the glue (Fig. 56).

(n) Repair other punctures if they have occurred (e.g., when a nail goes through both sides of the tube).

(o) If you don't have a spare tube

Fig. 54: Roughen the area around the leak with sandpaper.

Fig. 55: Apply a few drops of patch cement around the leak, rub it flat with your finger, and let it get tacky.

Fig. 56: Remove a patch cover and apply the patch over the patch cement.

and you have a massive tube split (Fig. 57), try using multiple overlaid patches to cover the rip. Wrap duct or electrician's tape around the tube over the patches. This patch job will probably leak but it may get you as far as a bike shop with repeated use of the tire pump.

Fig. 57: Use a rubber patch, then a canvas patch or duct tape over this bad puncture until you can install a new tube. *(Courtesy Schwinn Bicycle Company)*

(p) Inspect the tire inside and out for embedded glass, nails, or anything else that caused the puncture, then remove them (Fig. 58). Cover tire cuts with a canvas patch from your patch kit—or with a piece of duct or electrician's tape—so the cut itself won't pinch the tube as the tire flexes, possibly causing another flat. Install a new tire as soon as possible.

(q) Remove the rim strip (Fig. 59) and check the wheel for protruding spokes that may have punctured the tube. If you don't have a file to smooth the protruding spoke down as far as its nipple, cover it with a couple of patches or tape, replace the rim strip, and then at the first opportunity file it down or snip it off.

Fig. 58: Inspect the tire for cuts and embedded foreign particles before reassembling the tube and tire on the rim.

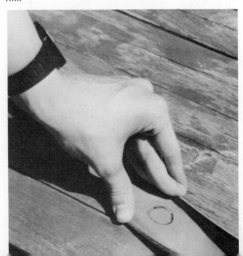

(r) Place the tube inside the tire and add two or three pump strokes of air to the tube.

(s) Place the tire over the wheel rim with the valve in the valve hole (Fig. 60).

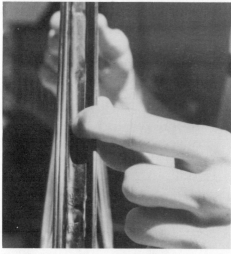

Fig. 59: Remove the rim strip to check for protruding spokes that could puncture the tube. Snip off any spokes that protrude above the nipple.

Fig. 60: After placing the tube in the tire and the tire over the rim, put the valve in the valve hole.

(t) Push one side of the tire onto the rim with your fingers (Fig. 61).

(u) Starting at the valve, push the other side of the tire on the rim. Work around the tire, alternating from one side of the valve to the other (Fig. 62). Use your fingers if possible. If you use a tire lever, be sure the tube is well inside the tire before using it. Be careful not to pinch the tube between the tire lever and the wheel rim, causing another puncture.

(v) Push the valve partway up into the tire.

(w) Squeeze the walls of the tire on both sides of the valve so that the

Fig. 61: Start replacing the tire on the rim by pushing one side of the tire all the way around the rim.

Fig. 62: Finish replacing the tire by using fingers and thumbs to work the other side of the tire on the rim. Use a tire lever carefully so you don't pinch the tube.

entire tire bead is seated in the rim, including the thicker section around the base of the valve.

(x) Pump the tube up about halfway. Inspect the tire on both sides to make sure the bead is seated in the rim. If you see any bulges, push the tire bead down so it sits securely in the rim. Pump the tube up the rest of the way.

(aa) Hold the pump on the valve as shown in Fig. 63 as you pump.

(bb) Punch the pump straight down with the side of your fist (Fig. 64) to remove it from the valve. *Note:*

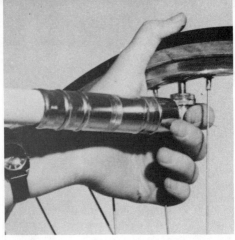

Fig. 63: Hold the pump as shown so you don't bend or break the valve. This is particularly important on fragile Presta valves.

Fig. 64: Remove the pump by punching it down. Don't wiggle the pump off a Presta valve or you'll break it.

On the more fragile Presta valves, it's important to hold and remove the pump as shown in Figs. 63 and 64 to avoid breaking off the valve.

(cc) Insert the wheel in the dropouts, then turn the quick-release lever to the closed position or tighten the axle bolts clockwise.

Caution: The quick-release mechanism is NOT a nut-and-bolt mechanism—it is a cam-actuated device. Properly tightened, the quick-release holds the wheel securely in the dropouts. Improperly tightened, the wheel could come out of the dropouts and cause an accident when you hit a bump. Tighten a quick-release by first turning the lever to the open position (Fig. 65). Hold this lever while you turn the quick-release adjusting nut on the other side of the hub BY HAND, NOT WITH A WRENCH, clockwise as far as possible. The (cont. on p. 74)

Fig. 65: The quick-release lever is in the open position. Adjust locking tension by holding the lever in this position while you *hand turn* the adjusting nut on the opposite side of the hub clockwise.

quick-release is properly adjusted when you begin to feel resistance as the lever is turned toward the closed position (Fig. 66). You should feel much resistance by the time the lever is in the closed position, pointing toward the rear of the bicycle (Fig. 67).

Fig. 66: You should feel resistance as you turn the quick-release lever to the 12 o'clock position.

Fig. 67: You should feel great resistance as you force the quick-release lever to the closed position shown here. That way you will know the wheel is safely tight in the dropouts.

PROBLEM 27: Flat rear tire.

Cause: Puncture.

Solution:

(a) Shift the chain to the small (high-speed) freewheel cog.

(b) Follow steps (a) through (f) in solution to Problem 26.

(c) Remove the rear wheel by shifting to the high gear, holding the derailleur back up so the chain clears the small freewheel cog, and simultaneously pull the wheel out of the dropouts.

(d) Repair the puncture by following steps (g) through (bb) in solution to Problem 26.

(e) Hold the derailleur out of the way and insert the rear wheel in the dropouts. Be sure the chain is on the small freewheel cog.

(f) Follow steps (cc) and (dd) in directions for Problem 26 above.

PROBLEM 28: The pump won't work.

Cause 1: A dent or bend in the pump tube.

Solution: If the dent or bend is near the pump head (the part that goes over the valve), you can still use the pump. Push the pump plunger only as far as the dent. It will take longer to pump up the tire, but at least you'll get it inflated.

If the dent or bend is farther up on the pump barrel:

(a) Unscrew the retainer nut at the pump end.

(b) Pull out the pump handle and plunger (one unit).

(c) Tap out the dent or bend with a wrench if the damage is light.

(d) Reassemble the pump. If you're lucky, you can repair the pump. If not, borrow a pump from a passing cyclist. If you're on the trail, far from a service station or bike shop, hide your bike if possible, hike out, and buy a new pump. Or push your bike back to civilization.

Cause 2: Dry pump plunger.

Solution:

(a) Disassemble the pump. See (a) and (b) above.

(b) Grease the plunger. If you don't have wheel grease, use some kind of spread or bacon fat.

(c) Reassemble the pump.

Cause 3: Wrong pump head.

Solution: If you have a skinny Presta valve but the pump has a Schrae-der valve head, you can screw a Presta valve adapter over the valve and use the Schraeder pump on the adapter. That's if you have one or can borrow one. If you *don't* have that adapter, you simply can't pump up the tire. See (d) in Cause 1 for possible solutions. But remember that you can't use a Presta pump head on a Schraeder valve or vice versa.

STEERING PROBLEMS

Front-wheel shimmy is a major cause of loss of control and serious accidents. Once it starts, side-to-side movement of the wheel becomes faster and wider and is virtually impossible to control. What *is* possible to control are its causes. Remember, an annoying wheel wobble at low speed can dump you at high speed. If you feel looseness or shimmy from the front wheel at any speed, stop, look for the problem, and correct it. Headset bearings can loosen on any type of bike, but they are more likely to loosen on an all-terrain bicycle. If you hear or feel noise from the hubs, these bearings may be about to self-destruct unless you remove the actual source, such as sand in the bearings.

PROBLEM 29: Front wheel shimmy.

Cause 1: Loose headset bearings.

Solution: Check and adjust the headset bearings this way:

(a) Straddle the bike. Keep both feet on the ground, squeeze the front brake lever tightly, and hold onto the handlebars with your right hand.

(b) Rock the bike back and forth. If you feel looseness in the fork or hear clicking sounds from the headset bearings, the headset is loose. Watch the fork and headset adjustable cup; if they move, the headset is loose.

(c) The headset locknut ("A" in Fig. 68) and the adjustable cup ("B" in Fig. 68) take a 32mm wrench. Since these wrenches are long and

Fig. 68: If you have a pair of 32mm wrenches along, use them to adjust the headset bearings. See text.

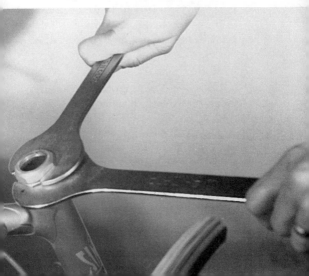

heavy, most cyclists leave them at home. Here's how to adjust the headset *without* them. (If you *do* have them, the same instructions apply. But if you are near a bike shop, have them adjust the headset.)

(d) If you have (or can borrow) two pairs of pliers or adjustable wrenches large enough to fit on the headset locknut and adjustable cup, hold the cup stationary while turning the locknut counterclockwise one or two turns. Do not remove the handlebars.

(e) Turn the adjustable cup by hand until it's tight.

(f) Hold the adjustable cup with one wrench and tighten the locknut with the other wrench (or pliers).

(g) Check the headset as in (a) and (b) above. If it's still loose, loosen the locknut and tighten the adjustable cup with a wrench or pliers until it is barely tight. Repeat step (f). Check the headset again and repeat these steps until all free play and looseness has been removed from the headset bearings.

(h) Lift the front wheel off the ground. Lean the bike to one side and then the other. The wheel should turn one way and then the other. If the wheels don't turn freely or the handlebars bind as they turn, the headset bearings are too tight. Turn the locknut one turn counterclockwise. Turn the adjustable cup counterclockwise a quarter turn. Hold the adjustable cup with one wrench and tighten the locknut with the other wrench. Check headset adjustment for looseness or tightness and readjust as necessary.

(i) If you do not have access to any tool that will fit on the 32mm headset locknut and adjustable cup, make this emergency adjustment until you can find the tools to make a more permanent adjustment: Fold your fist tightly around the adjustable cup and turn it clockwise. You should be able to turn it far enough to remove dangerous free play in the bearings. Repeat this step on the locknut. Then ride slowly and carefully, especially downhill, until you can find a garage or a bike shop equipped with the proper tools. Check the headset (as described above) frequently during the day and repeat this hand adjustment as necessary.

Cause 2: Loose non-sealed wheel bearings.

Solution: Readjust wheel bearings:

(a) Lift the front wheel off the ground and wiggle it from side to side. If you feel looseness, the bearings need adjusting. If the sideplay is moderate and you don't have special thin cone wrenches (Fig. 69), keep your speed low until you can get to a bike shop.

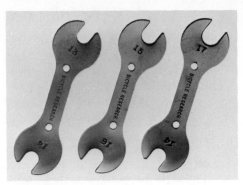

Fig. 69: Adjust loose hub bearings with a pair of thin hub cone wrenches. See text.

(b) If you have cone wrenches, hold the adjustable cone with one hub wrench while you loosen the locknut with another hub wrench (Fig. 69). Turn the locknut counterclockwise two turns.

(c) Turn the adjustable cone clockwise with the wrench until it's tight, then move it counterclockwise a half turn.

(d) Hold the cone with one wrench and tighten the locknut with the other wrench. Check for sideplay and remove further looseness by adjusting the hub bearings (as described above). Rotate the wheel until the tire valve is at approximately the two o'clock position and let go of the wheel. The weight of the valve should turn the wheel; if the wheel does not move, the hub bearings are too tight and should be readjusted by loosening the locknut, loosening the cone a half turn, and, while holding the cone, re-tightening the locknut. Make further bearing adjustments as necessary till the wheel turns freely and without sideplay. Twist the axle between thumb and forefinger, and if you feel roughness, see Problem 37.

Cause 3: Loose carriers or loose panniers.

Solution:

(a) Tighten carrier mounting bolts (Fig. 70).

Fig. 70: Tighten loose carrier bolts where the carrier is mounted to the bike frame, such as at points "A" and "B".

(b) Tighten pannier holding straps on the carrier.

(c) Tighten pannier straps holding the pannier load (if your panniers have such straps). These are the straps that fasten around the front of the pannier.

Cause 4: Unbalanced load, improper weight distribution.

Solution: Distribute weight evenly on both sides of the bicycle and over both wheels (Fig. 71). The load inside panniers should be tightly packed and restrained so it does not shift as you ride.

Cause 5: Bent fork or frame.

Fig. 71: Distribute weight evenly between the front and rear of the bicycle to avoid wheel shimmy.

Solution: You won't be able to straighten a bent frame on the road, but you can make these checks to see if the frame or fork is bent:

(a) Inspect the areas where the tubes are joined (Fig. 72). If the paint or chrome is wrinkled, the frame is buckled at that point.

(b) Check and if necessary align both wheels. See directions for Problem 2.

(c) Loosen the front wheel quick release lever or axle bolts and align the wheel in the dropouts so the wheel rim is the same distance from each fork blade.

(d) Spin the wheel. It should remain at the same distance from each fork blade as it rotates. If not, a fork blade is bent.

Fig. 72: Look for evidence of a bent frame, such as paint wrinkles where the tubes meet.

(e) Repeat this test with the rear wheel. The wheel should remain at the same distance from both the chainstays and the seatstays. If not, one of the stays or a main frame member is bent.

(f) If you find the fork or frame bent, ride *very* carefully and slowly to the nearest bike shop and have the frame straightened. If the frame is buckled too badly you may have to scrap the frame, remove all parts, and install them on a new frame when you get home.

PROBLEM 30: Loose handlebars.

Cause 1: A loose stem expander bolt.

Solution:

(a) Tighten the expander bolt (Fig. 73). You will need a 4, 5, or 6mm Allen wrench or a 10, 11, or 12mm wrench, depending on the make of the stem.

(b) Check expander bolt tightness. Stand in front of the bike, holding the front wheel between your legs, and twist the handlebars. If the handlebars move but the wheel does not, retighten the expander bolt.

Cause 2: A loose handlebar binder bolt.

Solution: The handlebars rotate in the stem because the stem clamp bolt is loose. Tighten that bolt, then try to rotate the handlebars. If you can, tighten the clamp bolt again.

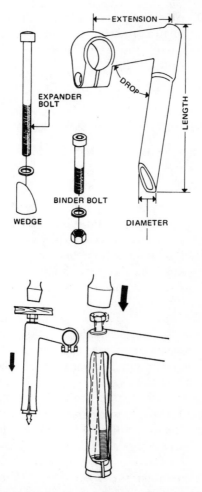

Fig. 73: Raise or lower the handlebars by loosening the stem expander bolt, then tapping it down as shown.

PROBLEM 31: The bicycle tends to steer itself to one side or the other.

Cause: Wheels are cocked at an angle in the dropouts.

Solution:
(a) Align the wheels in the dropouts. See instructions for Problem 2.
(b) Check the frame alignment. (See Problem 29.)

PROBLEM 32: Your hands or back hurt.

Cause 1: The handlebars are too high or too low.

Solution:
(a) *If you're riding a road bike,* loosen the stem expander bolt four or five turns counterclockwise.
(b) Put a piece of wood on the bolt head and tap it with a hammer (or a rock). You can now raise or lower the handlebars.

Caution: Leave at least 2½ inches of the stem inside the steering tube. Otherwise the stem could snap in two as you strain uphill, causing an accident.

(c) Tighten the expander bolt.
(d) *If you're riding an all-terrain bike,* you can raise or lower the handlebars on most models, but you must readjust the front brake shoe-to-rim clearance after adjusting the handlebar height. (See Problem 1.)

Cause 2: Hard handlebar tape.

Solution:
(a) Install a softer handlebar tape, such as Spenco grips, when you can.
(b) Meanwhile, tape anything soft, such as a piece of foam padding, on the handlebar scrap.

Cause 3: Thin gloves.

Solution: Buy gloves with more padding in the palm. Meanwhile, as you ride, keep changing hand positions on the handlebars to relieve constant pressure in one place.

WHEEL PROBLEMS

PROBLEM 33: Broken front wheel spoke.

Cause 1: Impact with a hard object, such as a curb.

Cause 2: A loose spoke is subject to whip movement that causes metal fatigue and spoke breakage, usually at the hub end of the spoke.

Solution 1 (to Causes 1 and 2):
(a) Remove bottom half of the broken spoke from the hub.
(b) Remove the wheel. (See Problem 26.)
(c) Remove the tire and rim strip.
(d) Remove the top half of the spoke.
(e) Install a new spoke, realign the wheel as described in Problem 2, and replace the wheel in the fork.

Solution 2: If you do not have a spare spoke:
(a) Follow steps (a) through (d).
(b) Realign the wheel as shown in instructions for Problem 2 and Fig. 13. You may have to readjust brake shoe-to-rim clearance if a brake shoe rubs on the rim. You should be able to get by until you can obtain a replacement spoke.

Cause 3: Extra heavy load and/or rider.

Solution:
(a) On an emergency basis, replace the spoke or realign the wheel as in Solutions 1 and 2, and in Problem 2.
(b) When you can, buy or build a new wheel with 40 spokes. Save the old one for casual town riding.

PROBLEM 34: Broken rear wheel spoke (not on freewheel side).

Causes: Same as Causes 1, 2, and 3 in Problem 33.

Solutions: Same as in Problem 33.

PROBLEM 35: Broken rear wheel spoke on free-wheel side.

Causes: Same as those in Problem 33.

Solution 1: If you have a spare spoke:
(a) Remove the rear wheel. (See Problem 27.)
(b) Follow steps (a) through (d) in Problem 33.
(c) You won't be able to replace the broken spoke with a new one without removing the freewheel or without making a special spoke as described below. You can't remove the freewheel without those special tools which are too heavy and cumbersome to carry on a trip. The solution is to snip off or pound down the flat head of a spoke with a hammer, tool, or rock so it will fit into the hub spoke hole on the freewheel side of the hub.
(d) Bend the head end of the spoke upward into a *J* shape.
(e) Hook the *J* end of the spoke into the spoke hole behind the freewheel.

(f) Insert the threaded end into the rim, thread on the nipple, and realign the wheel as in solution to Problem 2.

Solution 2: If you don't have a spare spoke:

(a) Follow steps (a) through (d) in Problem 33.
(b) Realign the wheel as described in Problem 2—unless you are carrying a heavy load, in which case follow step (c).
(c) Remove a spoke from the front wheel, realign the wheel, and install that spoke on the rear wheel as shown in solutions to Problems 33 and 35.

PROBLEM 36: A dented rim (wheel thumps as it turns).

Cause: The wheel has struck a pothole, curb, or other obstruction.

Solution:

(a) Realign the wheel as in solution to Problem 2.
(b) If the dent is so severe you can't pull it out by adjusting the spoke tension, ride slowly and carefully to the nearest bike shop and replace the rim. Remember, a badly dented rim affects steering and could cause an accident.

PROBLEM 37: Grinding sounds coming from hubs.

Cause 1: Sand or dirt in *non-sealed-bearing hubs*. If you've been riding on sand or dirt roads, these abrasives can work their way into the bearings.

Solution:
(a) Remove the wheel.
(b) Spin the axle between thumb and forefinger to feel for roughness.
(c) If bearings feel rough, remove the axle locknut, washer, and adjustable cup from the axle. (See Problem 29, Cause 2.)
(d) Put a rag under the hub to catch loose ball bearings.
(e) Remove the axle, ball bearings, and seals.
(f) Clean dirt, sand, and old grease from the bearings, cones, and hub.
(g) Regrease the bearings and reassemble the hub. If you don't have spare grease along, use motor or salad oil or bread spread until you can buy grease. Any lubricant is better than having abrasives scraping away and ruining the finely polished surfaces of your good hubs. Don't ride more than 50 miles on salad oil if you can avoid it, however. You can go on indefi-

nitely if you squirt oil into the hubs every 50 miles (on a road trip) or every 25 miles (on a mountain trail ride), but lubricate the hubs as soon as possible with a good grease such as Phil Wood or Lubriplate.

(h) Adjust hub bearings as in Problem 29, Cause 2.

Cause 2: Dirt or sand in *sealed-bearing hubs.*

Solution:

(a) Remove the wheel.

(b) Pry off the outer bearing seal with a sharp knife.

(c) Clean out as much of the bearing as you can see.

(d) Stuff fresh grease into the bearing. Push the grease in with your finger so that it penetrates to the inner side of the bearing.

(e) Replace the seal.

(f) Replace the wheel.

Note: The freewheel blocks access to the bearing on the right side of the rear wheel. As soon as possible, remove the freewheel and the bearing seal, then clean and grease the bearing.

PROBLEM 38: Broken quick-release skewer.

Cause: Metal fatigue. A rare occurrence, fortunately, but it does happen.

Solution: You cannot ride your bicycle unless the wheel is firmly held in the dropouts. Here's what to do if the *front wheel* skewer breaks:

(a) Remove the quick-release skewer. Save the pieces if you got hurt when the wheel came out of the dropouts.

(b) Remove both axle locknuts from the hub axle. (See Cause 2, Problem 29.)

(c) Put the wheel back in the fork dropouts.

(d) Squeeze the fork blades so you can thread on the axle locknuts. (You may have to hold the fork blades in the squeezed position with a pedal strap or rope.)

(e) Thread on the axle locknuts, but do not tighten them.

(f) Check the wheel for wobble and sideplay as in Problem 29, Cause 2. Readjust one adjustable cone as necessary before tightening the locknuts.

(g) Tighten the axle locknuts.

(h) *Pedal slowly and carefully until you can install a new quick-release unit.*

(i) *If the rear wheel skewer breaks,* do not attempt this solution unless the rear dropouts are vertical. If the dropouts are horizontal—as on most bicycles—you can't tighten the locknuts so that they will keep the wheel from sliding in the drop-outs. My advice is to walk the bike until you can find and install a new quick release.

PROBLEM 39: A bent axle.

Cause: The wheel hits a bump, hard. It's more likely to occur when carrying a heavy load.

Solution 1:
(a) Remove the wheel.
(b) If the axle is not bent too far, you can readjust hub bearings as in Problem 29, Cause 2, to remove axle binding due to the bent axle.
(c) You probably won't be able to adjust the bearings so that the wheel spins without some binding, but at least you will be able to ride the bike. The wheel will be tight in some places and loose in others. So ride carefully until you can replace the bent axle with a new one.
(d) The axle may be bent so badly that a hub bearing adjustment that permits the wheel to turn also permits dangerous wheel wobble. In that case, I advise you to walk the bike to the nearest bike shop for a new axle. If you are far from a bike shop, you may be able to ride *very* slowly, not over five or six miles per hour, to the nearest bike shop.

PROBLEM 40: A wheel is loose in the dropouts.

Cause 1: The quick-release mechanism is not correctly and safely tightened.

Solution: See Problem 29, Cause 5 for instructions on the use of the quick-release mechanism.

Cause 2: Axle bolts are not safely tightened.

Solution: Tighten these bolts firmly.

PROBLEM 41: The wheel wobbles from side to side.

Cause: Loose wheel bearings.

Solution: See Problem 29, Cause 2.

PEDALING PROBLEMS

PROBLEM 42: The chain, cranks, and pedals turn, but the bike won't move.

Cause: Dirt is holding the freewheel pawls open.

Solution:
(a) Tilt the bicycle to one side, free-wheel up.
(b) Squirt or spoon about an ounce of kerosene into the freewheel bearings (arrow, Fig. 74). *Do not spill solvent on the tire!*

Fig. 74: Squirt a solvent such as kerosene into the freewheel bearings, arrow, to remove dirt that's holding the pawls open. See text.

(c) Lift the rear wheel and turn the cranks backward and forward to loosen whatever is holding the pawls open.

(d) Squirt *light* oil into the freewheel.

PROBLEM 43: A pedal feels loose.

Cause 1: The pedal has become unscrewed in the crank.

Solution: Tighten the pedal. Pedals *always* thread on in the direction of crank rotation. The right pedal threads on clockwise, the left pedal threads on counterclockwise. *Do not ride with a pedal loose in a crank.* The crank is aluminum, the pedal axle is steel. A loose pedal can strip pedal threads in the crank, leading to an expensive crank replacement.

Cause 2: Loose pedal bearings.

Fig. 75: Adjust pedal bearings by first removing the dust cap.

Fig. 76: Loosen the pedal locknut so you can adjust the bearing cone.

Solution: Readjust the pedal bearings:
(a) Remove the dust cap (Fig. 75).
(b) Loosen the locknut two or three turns (Fig. 76).
(c) Turn the adjustable cone with a small screwdriver (Fig. 77) until it is just snug. Do not overtighten.

Fig. 77: Tighten or loosen the pedal adjustable cone as necessary. See text.

(d) Tighten the locknut.

(e) Check the pedal bearings by pushing the pedal up and down and in and out. If you still feel looseness, readjust as above.

(f) If the pedal feels tight as you turn it by hand, loosen the locknut, back off the adjustable cone a half turn, and tighten the locknut. Check bearing adjustment as instructed and make further adjustments as necessary until all bearing sideplay and tightness are removed and pedal turns smoothly.

(g) If the bearings look clean, replace the dust cap. If the bearings look dirty, remove the locknut, adjustable cone, and bearings. Clean the cups, cones, bearings, and axle, then regrease and reassemble the pedal. Adjust bearings as instructed.

Cause 3: A loose toe clip.

Solution: Tighten the two bolts and nuts that hold each toe clip on the pedal.

PROBLEM 44: The crank feels loose.

Cause 1: A loose crank binder bolt.

Solution: A loose crank will soon round out the beveled square hole where it mounts on the bottom bracket axle (Fig. 78). The crank is aluminum, the bottom bracket axle is steel. If the crank hole becomes larger than the axle shaft, you will need a new crank, a costly solution. A better solution is to:

(a) Remove the crank dust cap.
(b) Tighten the crank with a 14 or 15mm socket wrench (depending on the make and model of the crank). Some cranks tighten with a 6mm Allen wrench (Fig. 79).

Fig. 78: Tighten the crank fixing bolt with a 14 or 15mm socket wrench.

Fig. 79: Tighten the crank fixing bolt on this style crank with a 6mm Allen wrench.

Note: Tighten the crank bolts every 50 miles for the first 200 miles on a new bike or after the crank has been removed and replaced.

Cause 2: Loose bottom bracket bearings.

Solution: Readjust bottom bracket bearings:

(a) Loosen the bottom bracket lockring with a lockring wrench (Fig. 80). If this wrench isn't in your tool kit, use a hammer (or anything heavy) and a screwdriver to turn the lockring a half to a full turn counterclockwise. (This is an emergency operation that can be avoided by overhauling the bottom bracket before the trip. Use the latter method carefully so you don't gouge the lockring.)

(b) Tighten the adjustable cup (Fig. 81) with a pin wrench or use the screwdriver and hammer approach, carefully. Tighten the cup until it's snug. Do not overtighten.

Fig. 80: Use a special wrench (or a hammer and screwdriver in a pinch) to loosen the bottom bracket lockring.

Fig. 81: Adjust the cup on a bottom bracket with a pin wrench or use a screwdriver edge. See text.

(c) Hold the adjustable cup with the pin wrench and tighten the lockring. If you don't have a pin wrench, use the hammer and screwdriver. If the adjustable cup turns as you tighten the lockring, loosen the lockring and adjustable cup a half turn and try again.

(d) Check the bottom bracket bearing adjustment by grasping each crank (use two hands) and rocking them back and forth. You should feel no looseness. If bearings are loose, readjust them as above.

(e) Slip the chain off the chainwheels and set it on the bottom bracket shell below the small chainwheel. Spin the cranks; they should turn smoothly, without binding.

(f) If the cranks are tight or bind, turn the lockring and the adjustable cup counterclockwise a half turn. Tighten the lockring and check the cranks as above. Make further bearing adjustments until the cranks turn smoothly.

PROBLEM 45: A toe or toe clip hits the front tire or fender on a sharp turn.

Cause: The frame is too short.

Solution 1:

(a) Remove the front fender if your foot strikes it while turning (Fig. 82). Otherwise your foot could get caught between the fender and the frame and cause an accident on a sharp turn.

Solution 2: If your foot hits the tire on a turn, the bike is *definitely* unsafe. The only solution I can offer is to return the bike, try to get your money back, and

Fig. 82: Remove the fender if it comes so close your foot can hit it on a sharp turn.

tell the seller why you are returning it. Meanwhile, try to avoid sharp turns, ride slowly, and take great care to keep your foot far enough back on the pedals to avoid hitting the tire.

PROBLEM 46: Your heel strikes the quick-release lever.

Cause: The quick-release lever is facing the front of the bike.

Solution: First, CAUTION! the quick release may be in the open position. See Problem 29, Cause 5 for proper adjustment and use of a quick-release mechanism. Make sure the quick-release lever is closed when it is facing the rear of the bicycle.

SADDLE PROBLEMS

PROBLEM 47: Saddle hurts.

Cause 1: Wrong saddle tilt.

Solution: Adjust saddle tilt. Excessive downward tilt throws the body forward and causes your bottom to slide onto the nose of the saddle. Excessive upward tilt shoves the body backward and causes your bottom to ride over the rear of the saddle.

(a) Loosen and adjust saddle tilt bolts (Fig. 83).
(b) Move the saddle until it is tilted slightly downward or is flat, parallel to the top tube.
(c) Make further tilt adjustments, upward or downward, until you find a comfortable position.

Cause 2: Wrong saddle height.

Solution: Adjust saddle height:
(a) Loosen the saddle binder bolt or the saddle quick release (Fig. 84)

Fig. 83: Adjust saddle tilt by loosening the saddle clamp bolts.

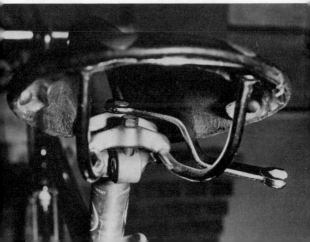

Fig. 84: Adjust the saddle height by loosening the quick-release mechanism or the standard binder bolt.

and move the saddle up or down as desired. See (b) below.

(b) The saddle is at, or close to, the correct height when, with your foot on a pedal that's at the five o'clock position (with the crank parallel to the downtube), your knee is slightly bent. *Note:* If the saddle is too low, your leg is not fully extended as you pedal, which puts excessive stress on the knee and causes knee pain and even knee damage. If the saddle is too high you will have difficulty mounting, dismounting, and reaching the pedals with your foot, all of which can cause loss of control and an accident.

(c) *Leave at least 2½ inches of the saddle inside the seat tube* to avoid breaking the seat post (Fig. 85).

Cause 3: A leather saddle has stretched and become swaybacked.

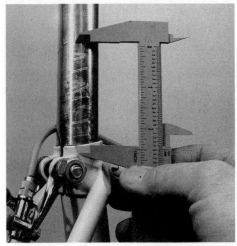

Fig. 85: Make sure *at least* 2½ inches of the seatpost is inside the seat tube.

Fig. 86: Remove saddle stretch by turning the stretch adjuster nut counterclockwise.

Solution 1: Remove saddle stretch.

(a) Underneath the nose of the saddle is a stretch adjuster nut (arrow in Fig. 86). Turn this nut counter-clockwise until the saddle is firm.

Solution 2: The saddle is new and/or not broken in:

(a) Apply a leather preservative such as neat's-foot oil or Brooks Proof-ide dressing when you can do it.

(b) The saddle needs breaking in, which takes time and a lot of riding. You could try soaking it in neat's-foot oil and pounding it with a baseball bat to soften it. It has been done.

Cause 4: Wrong saddle.

Solution: Change the saddle as follows:

(a) A plastic saddle will never get any

Fig. 87: Use a spring-mounted leather saddle like this one for greater protection against road shock.

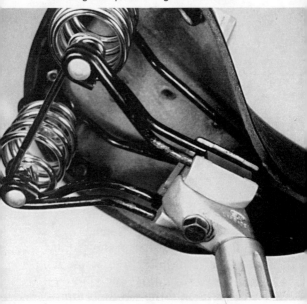

softer or more comfortable than the day it left the factory. If your saddle is plastic, I advise you to get a good leather saddle at the first opportunity. You could try a Spenco saddle cushion, which fits over the saddle, but a leather saddle is the best solution.

(b) You're a woman and the narrow man's leather saddle does not conform to your anatomy. Change to a wider leather saddle designed for women, such as the Brooks "S" saddle.

(c) Install a spring-mounted leather saddle (Fig. 87) which absorbs road shock much better than standard saddles.

CHAIN PROBLEMS

PROBLEM 48: The chain breaks.

Cause: Obvious.

Solution 1: Remove the broken link, pull the chain up by one more link and put the chain back together using the chain-breaker tool (Fig. 88).

(a) Turn the chain-breaker tool handle counterclockwise until you can fit the tool over the chain.

(b) Align the chain tool over a chain rivet.

(c) Turn the chain tool handle clockwise six turns.

(d) Remove the chain tool by turning the handle counterclockwise.

(e) The rivet should now be forced far enough out of the chain link so you can twist the chain apart with two hands. If not, use the chain tool and with one more turn push the rivet farther in. Leave a small sec-

Fig. 88: Use this chain breaker tool to push a chain rivet nearly out so you can remove the chain or shorten or lengthen it by removing or adding links.

tion of the rivet in the chain link to hold the chain together when you reinstall it.

Solution 2: If you're alone and without a chain breaker, and there's no chance of borrowing one from a passing cyclist . . . and you're far from a bike shop:

(a) Set the bike on the ground, derailleur side up. Find a nail on the ground or use a small screwdriver (or anything that's the same diameter or a bit smaller than the rivet) and with a rock, pound the rivet just far enough out of the broken link so you can remove it. Twist the chain so that it comes apart, but leave the rivet in the side plate so you can re-connect the chain.

(b) Turn the bike over so that the chain lies on the ground. Pull the chain up one link and pound the rivet back with the same "tool." Do not despair; you can do it. It has happened to me and I used a nail and a rock.

PROBLEM 49: The chain skips.

Solution 1: See Problems 11 and 22.

Solution 2: Lubricate the chain.

If you have had emergency road problems not covered in this book, I'd be delighted if you would write to tell me about them and how you solved the problem(s). Write me, Eugene A. Sloane, c/o Simon & Schuster, 1230 Avenue of the Americas, New York, New York 10020.

Good luck and Godspeed!